Table of Contents

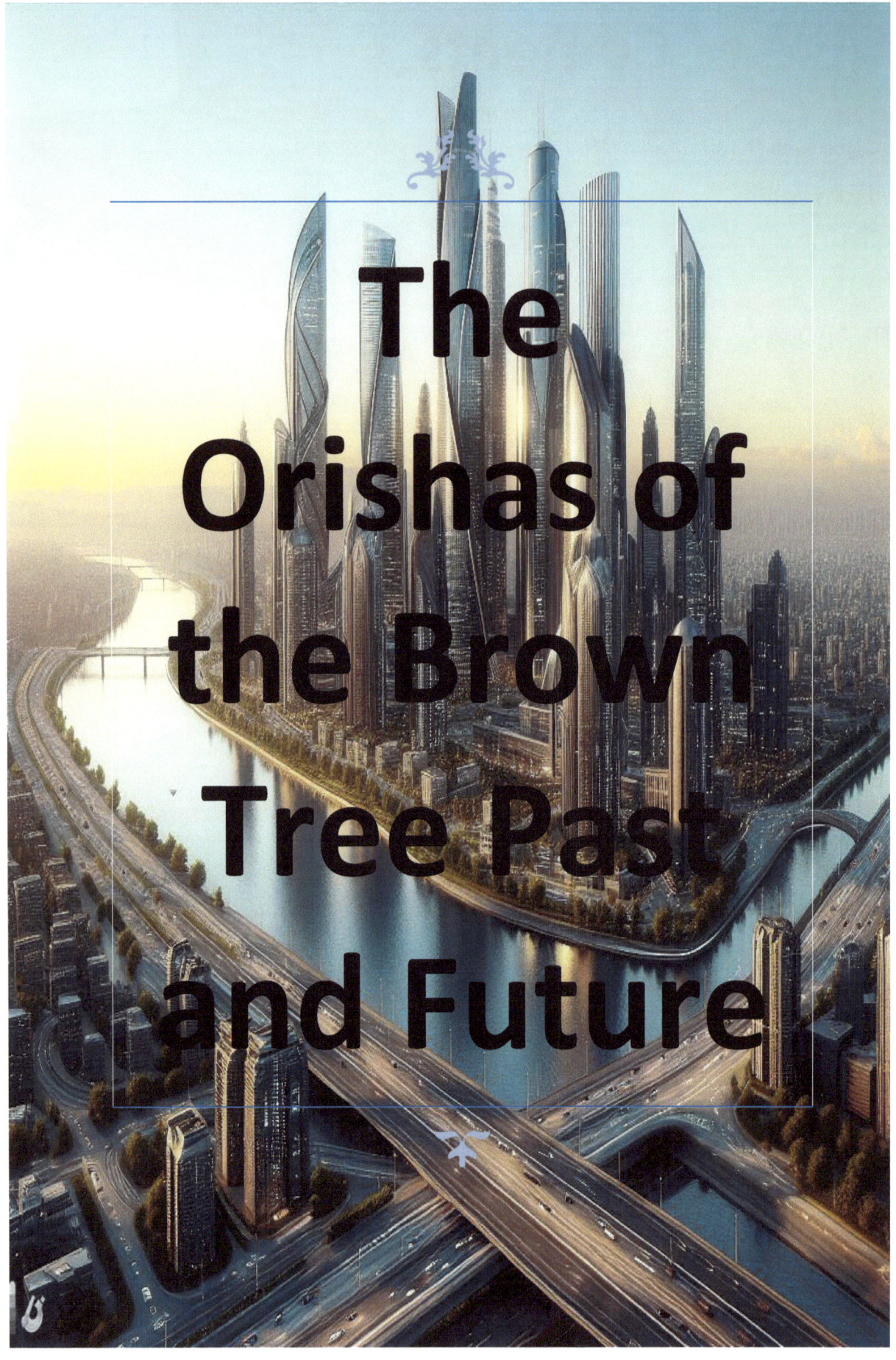

The Orishas of the Brown Tree Past and Future

This book is dedicated to my loving partner Randale Love. May our lives together always be an enlightening spiritual journey of love and happiness.

Elegua

Elegua, also known as Esau, Elegba or Legba, who knows all the languages spoken on earth, serves as a messenger between the gods and people. All messages need to be relayed through him but be careful he is a trickster god. He also loves children an babysits them as adults are talking. The door opener for some but some may come through a direct ancestor.

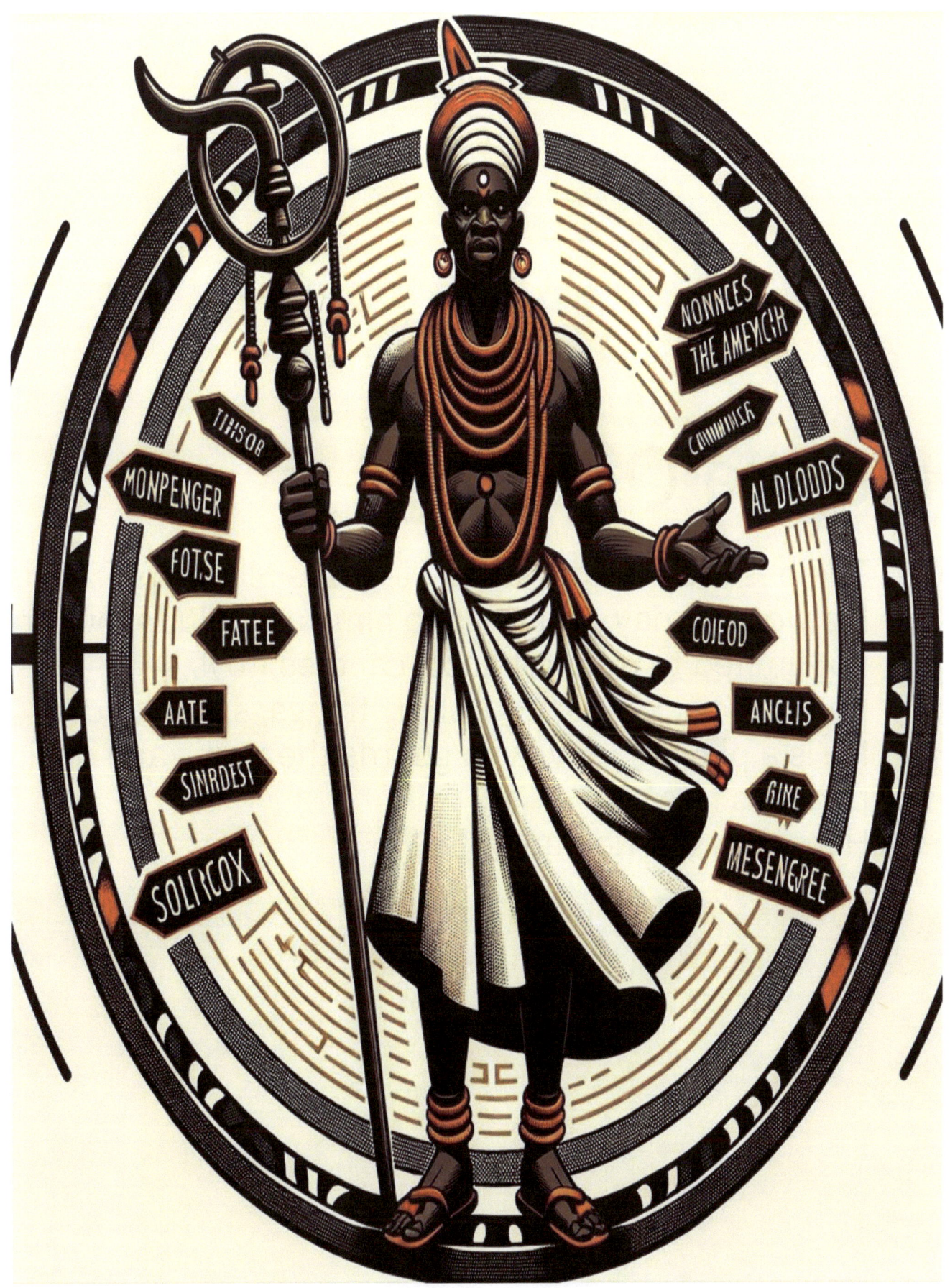

Elegua Offerings

The best day to contact to Elegua is Mondays. This is his worship day. Offerings to him can include, but are not limited to rum, tobacco, candies, toys, pennies/pocket change, shiny things, spicy foods.
He is a playful deity, who guards the paths and decides people's fate.
His colors are Red and Black.

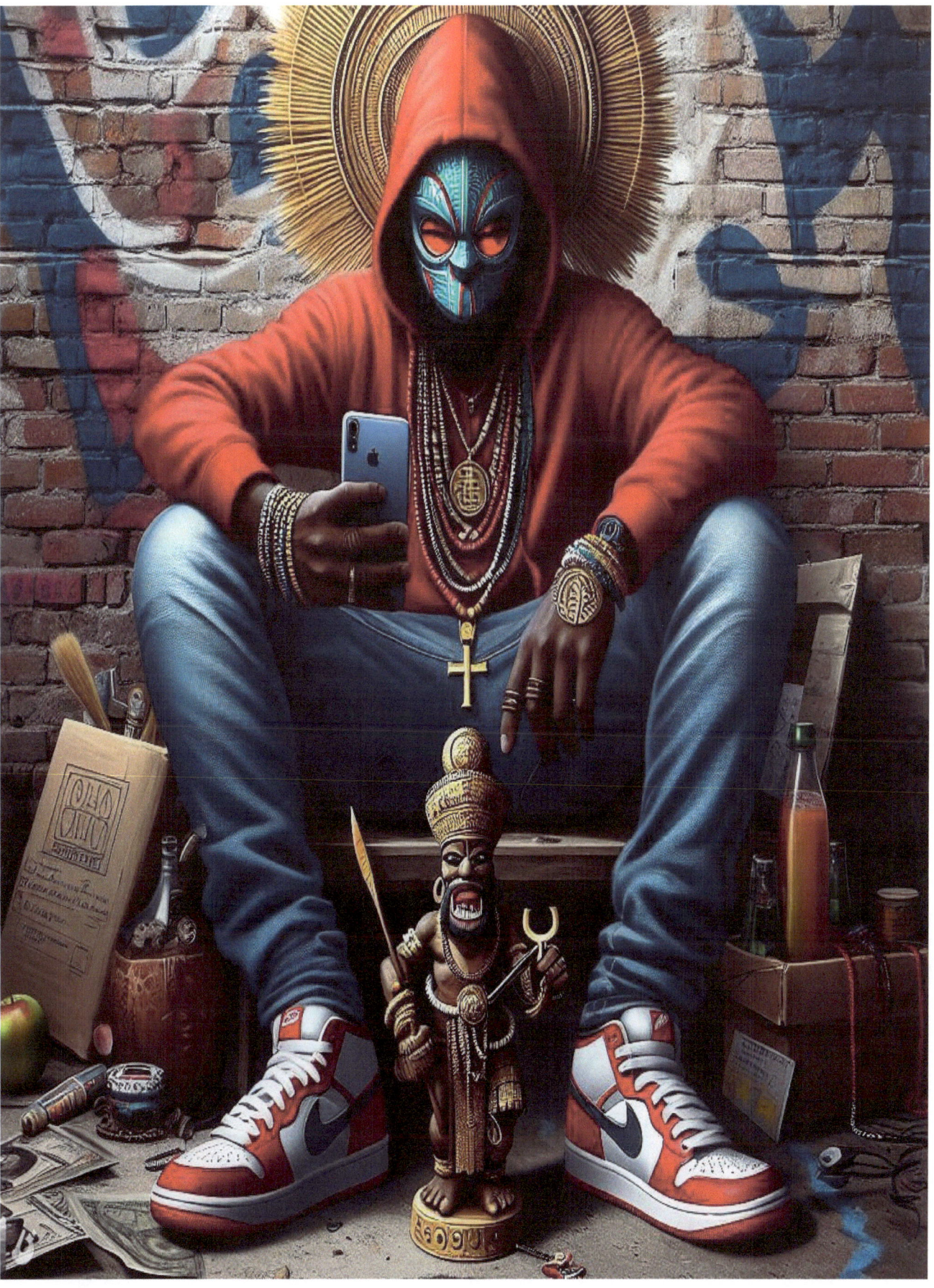

Yemaya: Queen of the Sea, Goddess of the Ocean

Yemaya is the mother of all Orisha's, Humanity and all Living things. She is a Goddess of fertility, love, protection, and healing. This Goddess has control over all the Oceans and Seas because it is believed it comes from, she. Yemoja Goddess of the New Year. Yemaya the Mermaid. She has an infinity for the color blue. Yemaya inspires individuals to tap into their own intuition for nurturing and finding strength in vulnerability

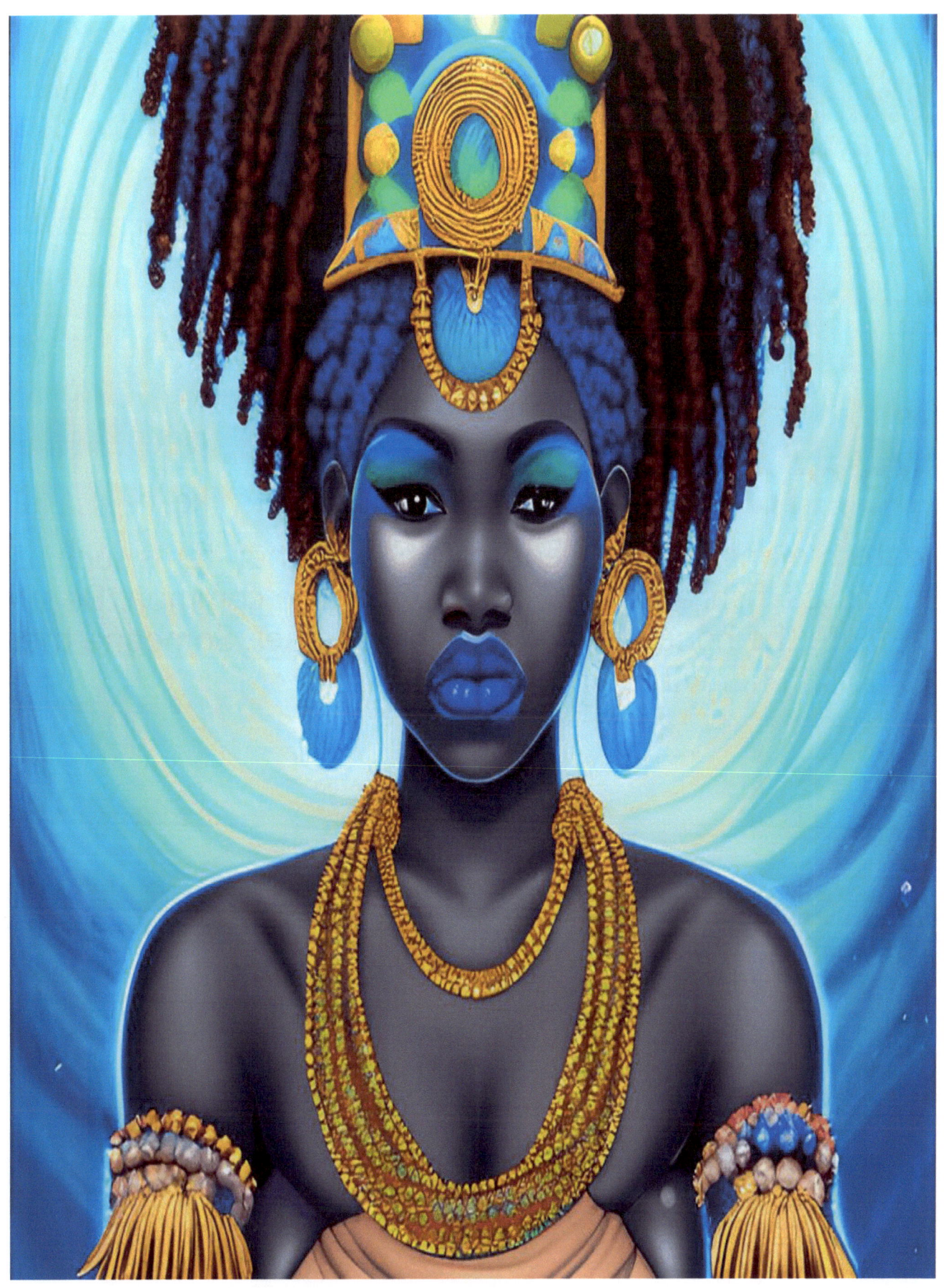

Yemaya's offerings include fruits like watermelons, oranges, and coconuts. Other items such as molasses, fish, and white flowers are also common. Be sure to taste the honey before offering it to her. Someone tried to poison her with tainted honey.

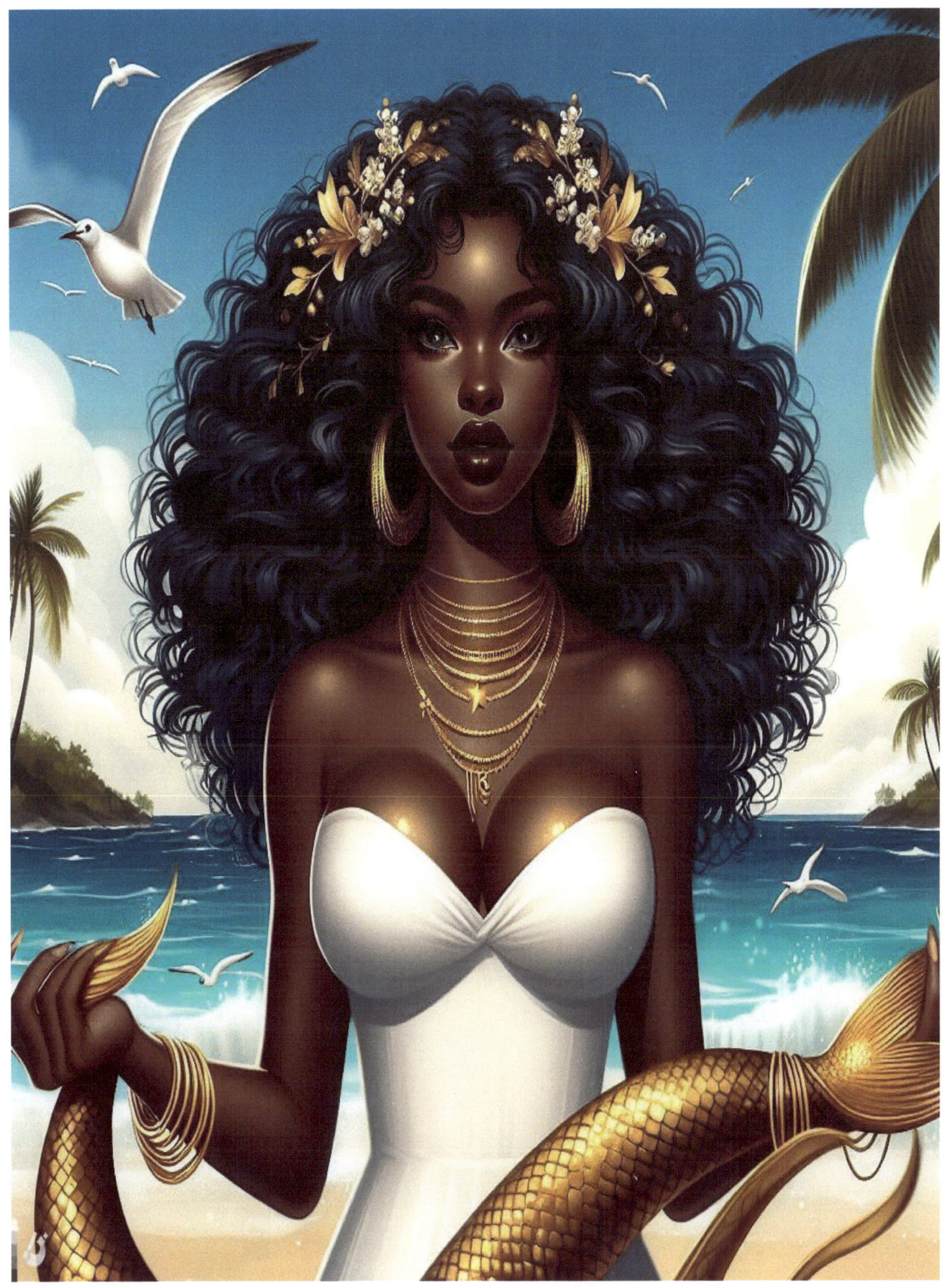

Oshun the River and Goddess of Love

Oshun (or Ochun) is the beloved Yoruba goddess of love. As such, she exudes the traits of love, sweetness, beauty, and sensuality. She has dominion over everything that flows, whether it is water, money, love, or a mother's milk. She is the granter of wishes, the grower of love, and the giver of laughter. She is always seen in the color yellow.

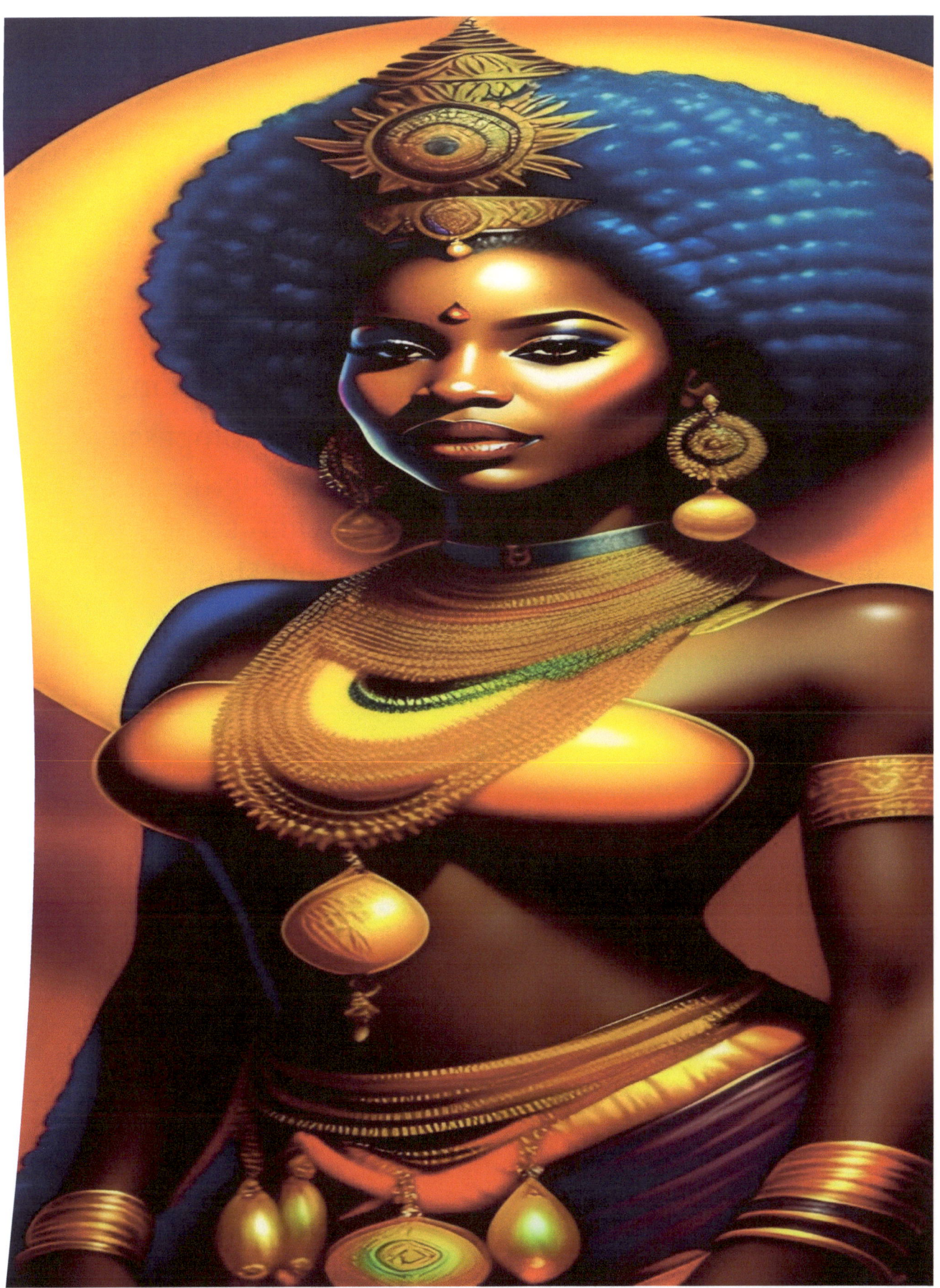

Oshun's beauty extends beyond physical appearance, embodying qualities like love, sensuality, and compassion. She encompasses both outer grace and inner strength.
Oshun's Offerings are subjects to beautify her: such as a mirror, makeup, comb, brush, perfume, jewelry, and sunflowers.
It is said that when setting your offering and creating spells setting them up near running water will increase them.

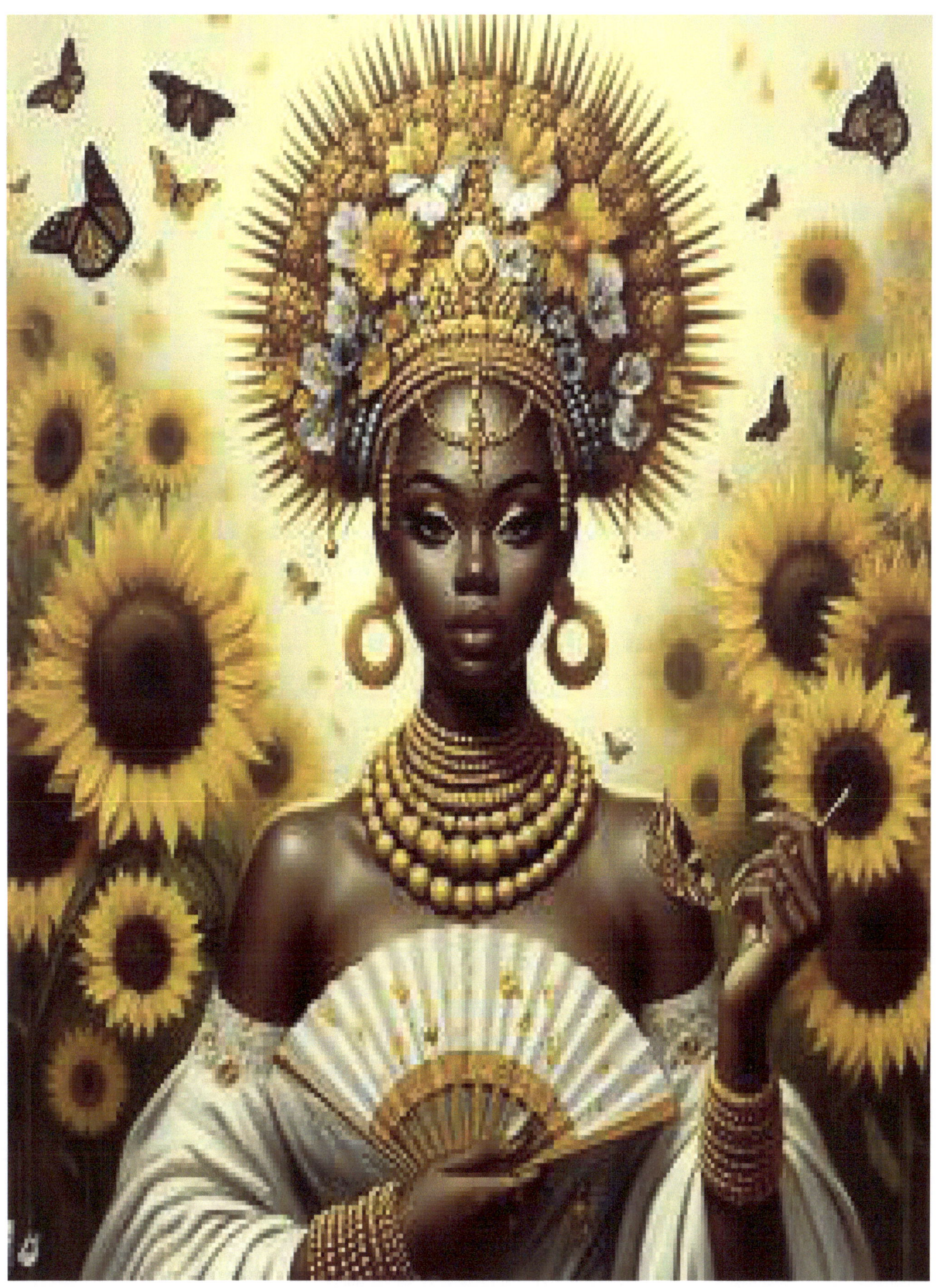

15

Obatala: The Orisha of Creation

Obatala is the oldest Orisha and is looked at as a father figure. He is the creator of humanity and is symbolic for knowledge and peace. Obatala is sometimes syncretized with Jesus Christ due to his association with creation, purity, and compassion. His color is white.

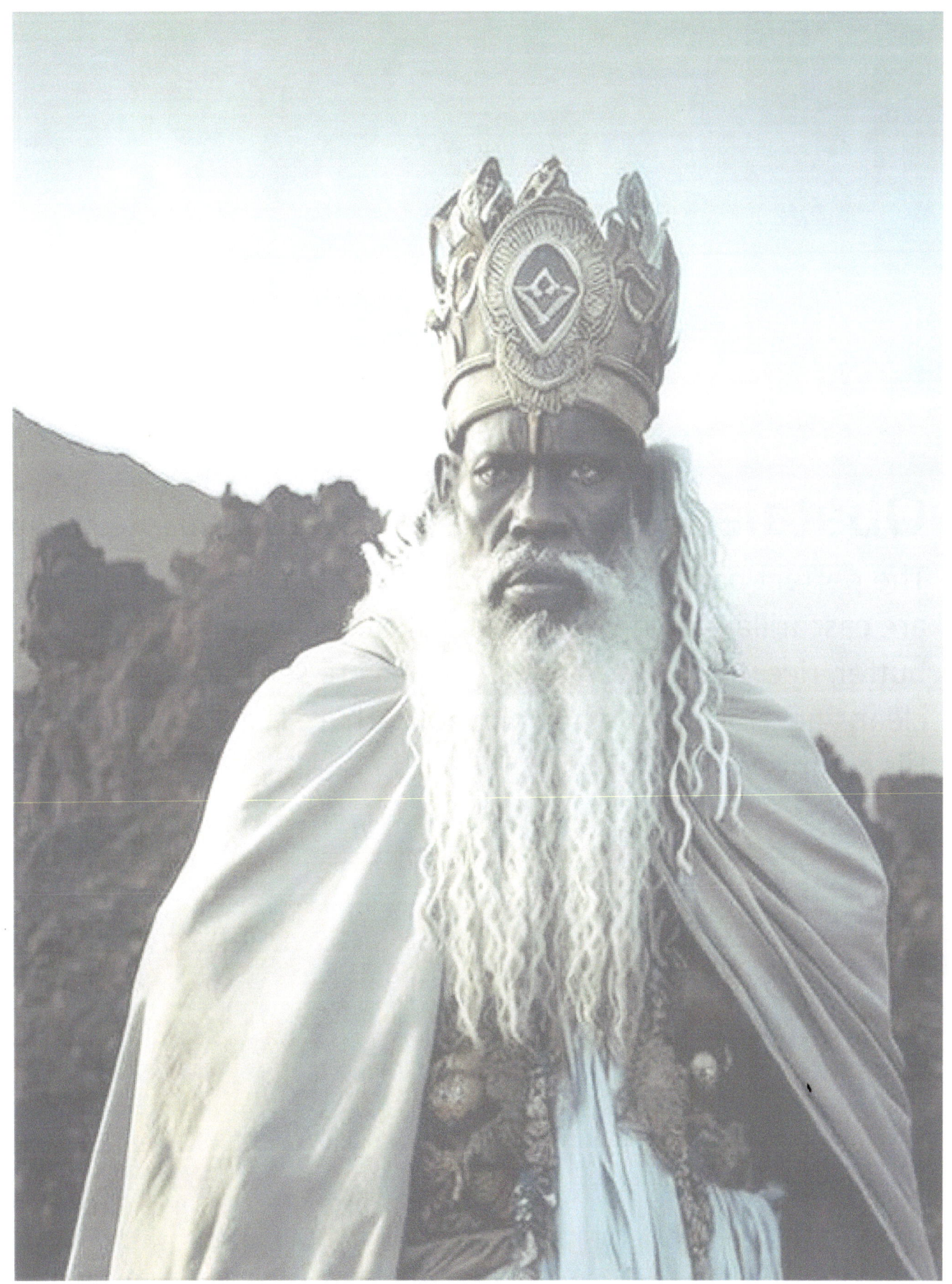

Obatala and Yemaya are seen as a divine married couple. The perfect balance. Yin, and Yang. Obatala's favorite offerings are cascarilla (powdered eggshells), sugar, water, milk, shea butter, rice, and white flowers, which are seen as pure and cleansing. Don't serve him alcoholic, there is a story behind it. His color is white.

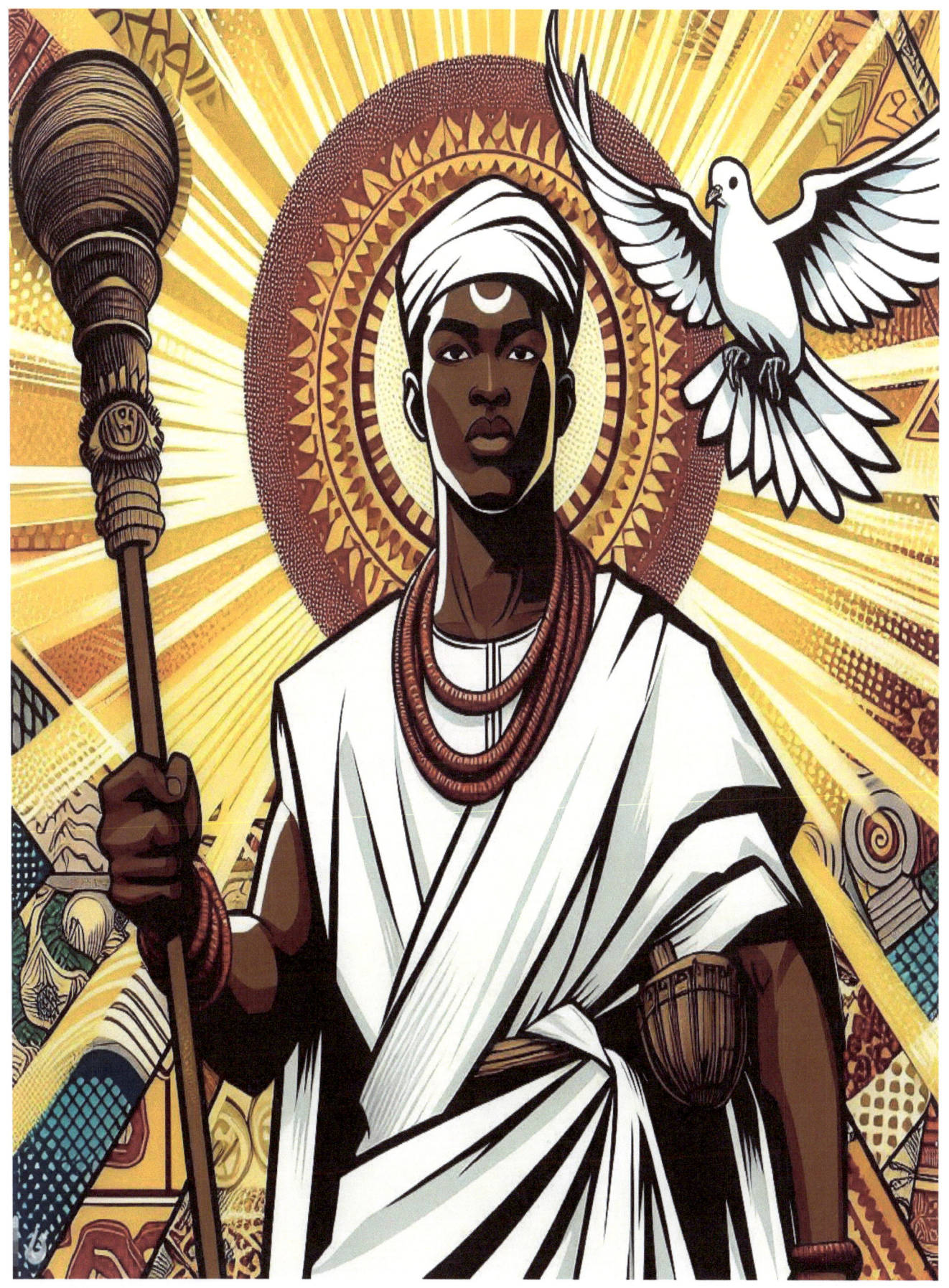

Shango: God of Thunder and Lightning

Shango (Chango) is known as the protection god. He is called upon for strength, guidance, and Justice. His presence is said to be felt with thunder followed by a bolt of lightning. Shango will bring upon change. His colors are red and white. Shango and Ogun are brothers, they have equal powers that are very similar and are both relative to energy.

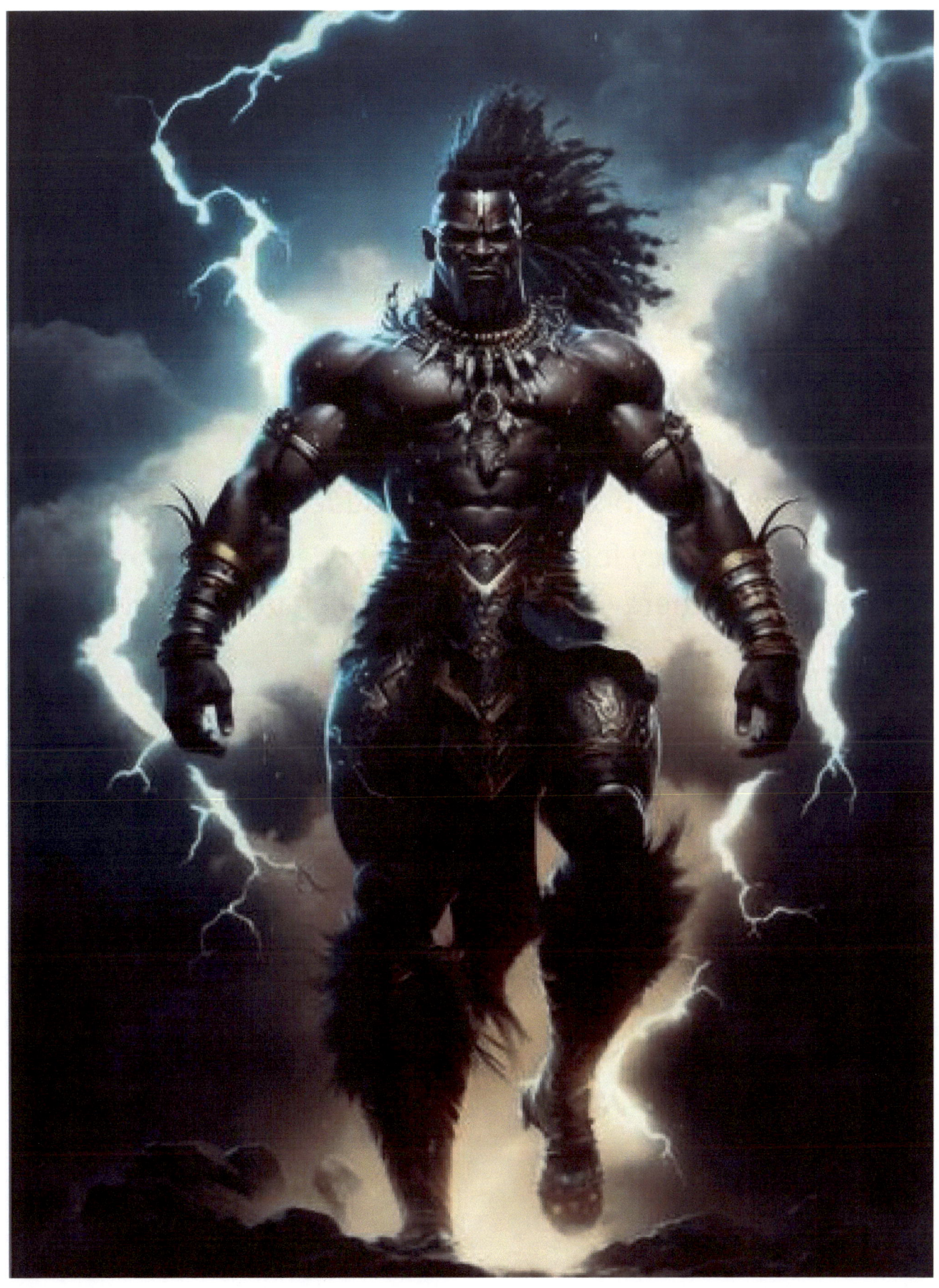

Shango's favorite offerings include liquor, sugar, copper, red foods, and spicy foods, which are believed to help strengthen his power and energy. His ceremonies include drums, music, and dance.

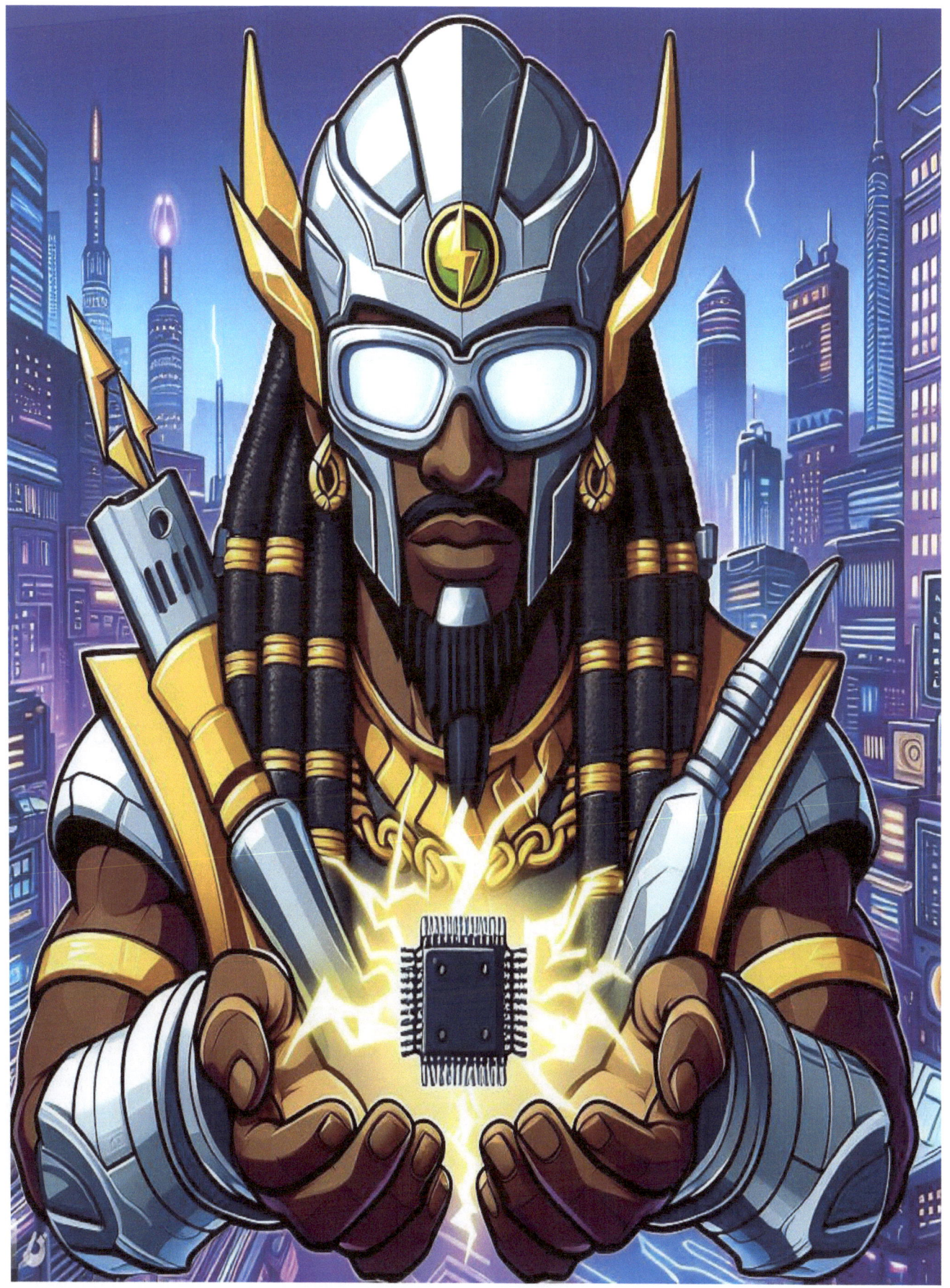

Oyá (Ya) The Orisha of the Winds

Oya (Yoruba: *Oya*, also known as Ya) is represented by winds, storms and lightening to represent her unpredictable personality. She is often seen with 2 swords or a machete. She is the guardian of cemeteries and the messenger between the living and dead, because of this Oya is the gatekeeper of secrets and the goddess of transformation. Her color is purple, some say red.

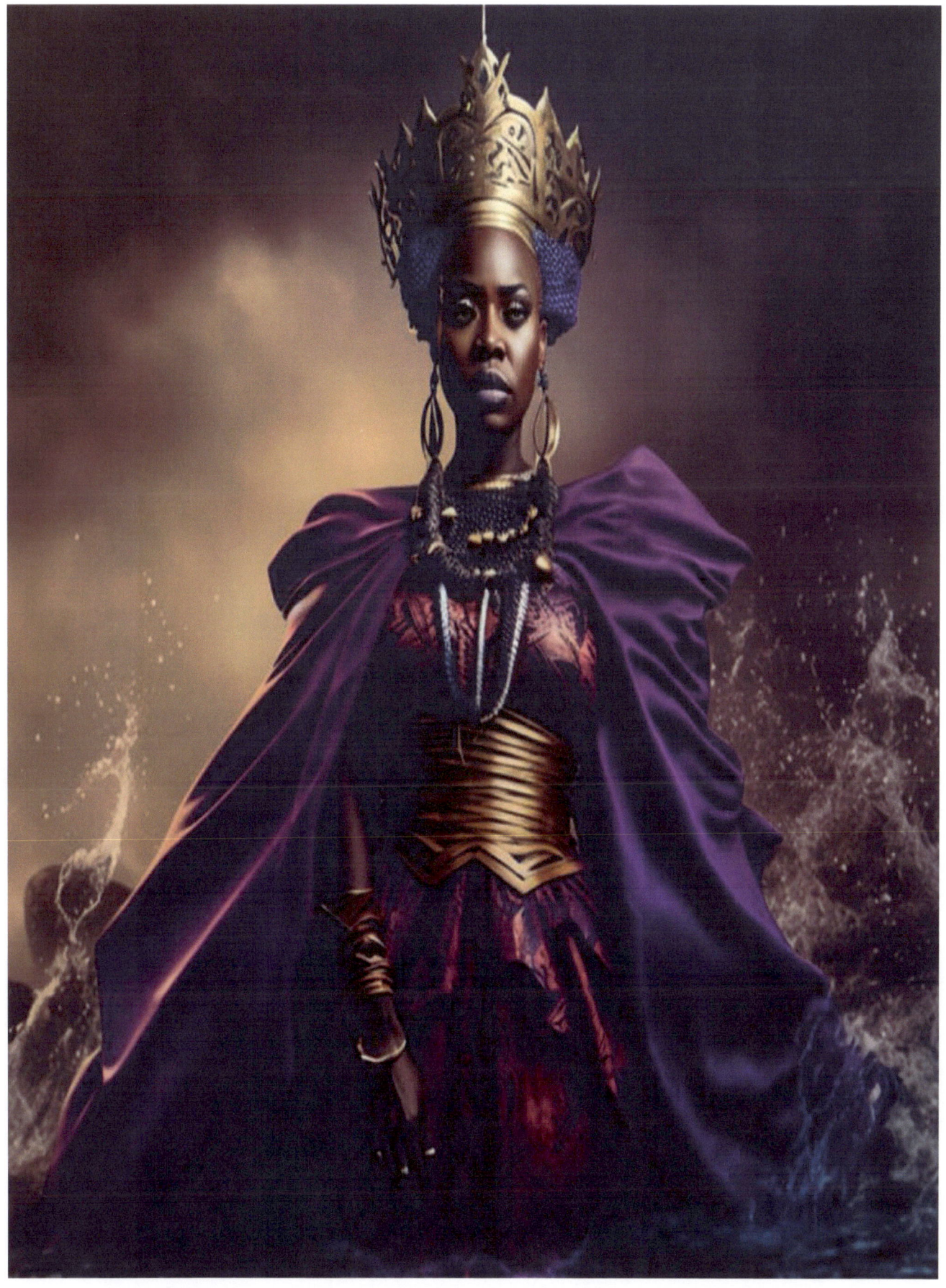

Oya is not specifically tied to the origination of the modern witches, but she is who they invoke when they try and communicate with the dead and use the speaks to the dead and the living, the elements of the earth for powers. Oya's favorite offerings include flowers, fruits, and wine, but she is also known for her love of eggplants, which are said to represent her power to transform and shape-shift.

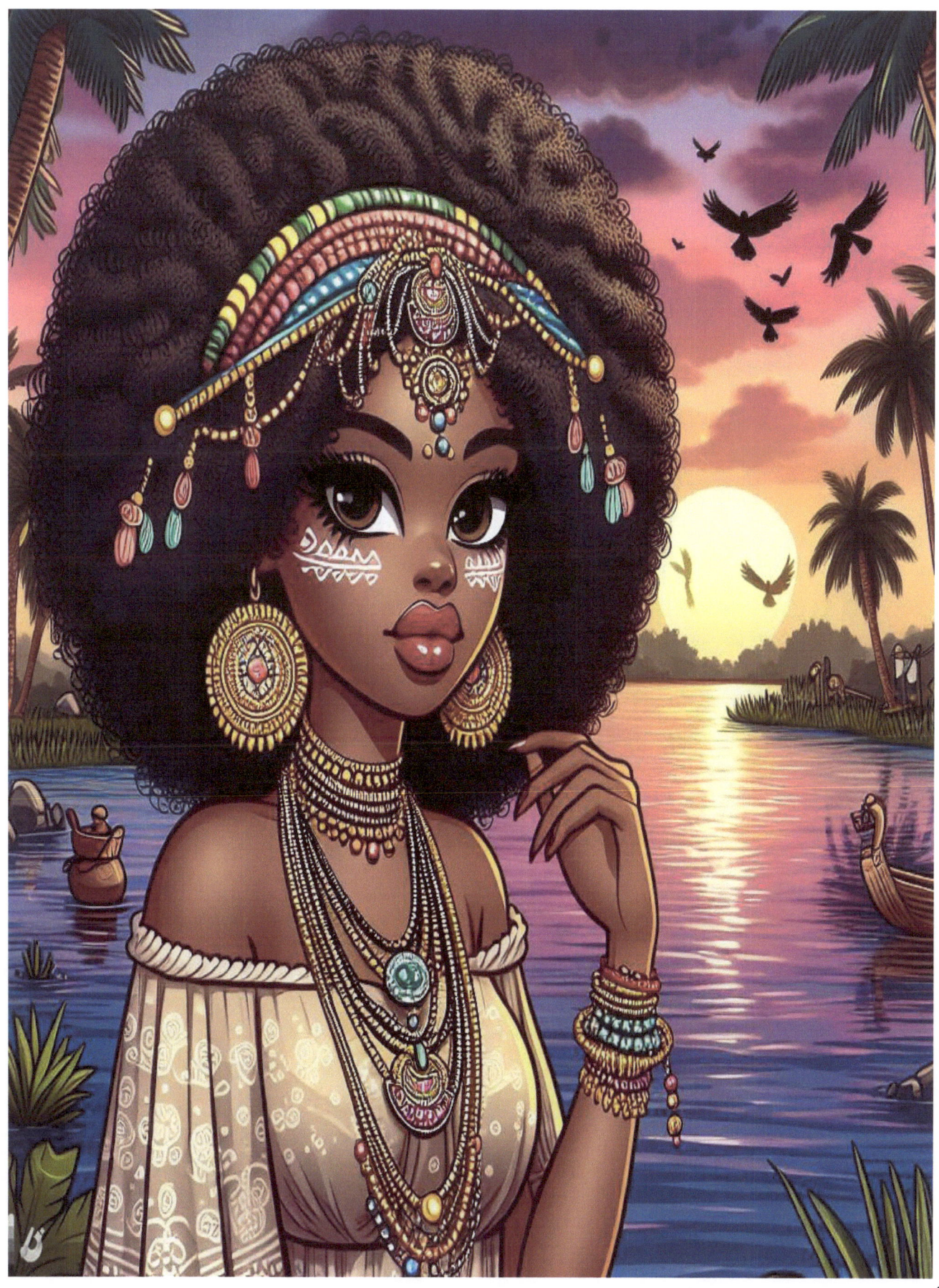

Ogun: The God of War

Even though Ogun is the God of war and is usually called upon for battle and metal weaponry, he is also known as a healer because he has the ability to transform negative energy into positive energy. His color is green and black.

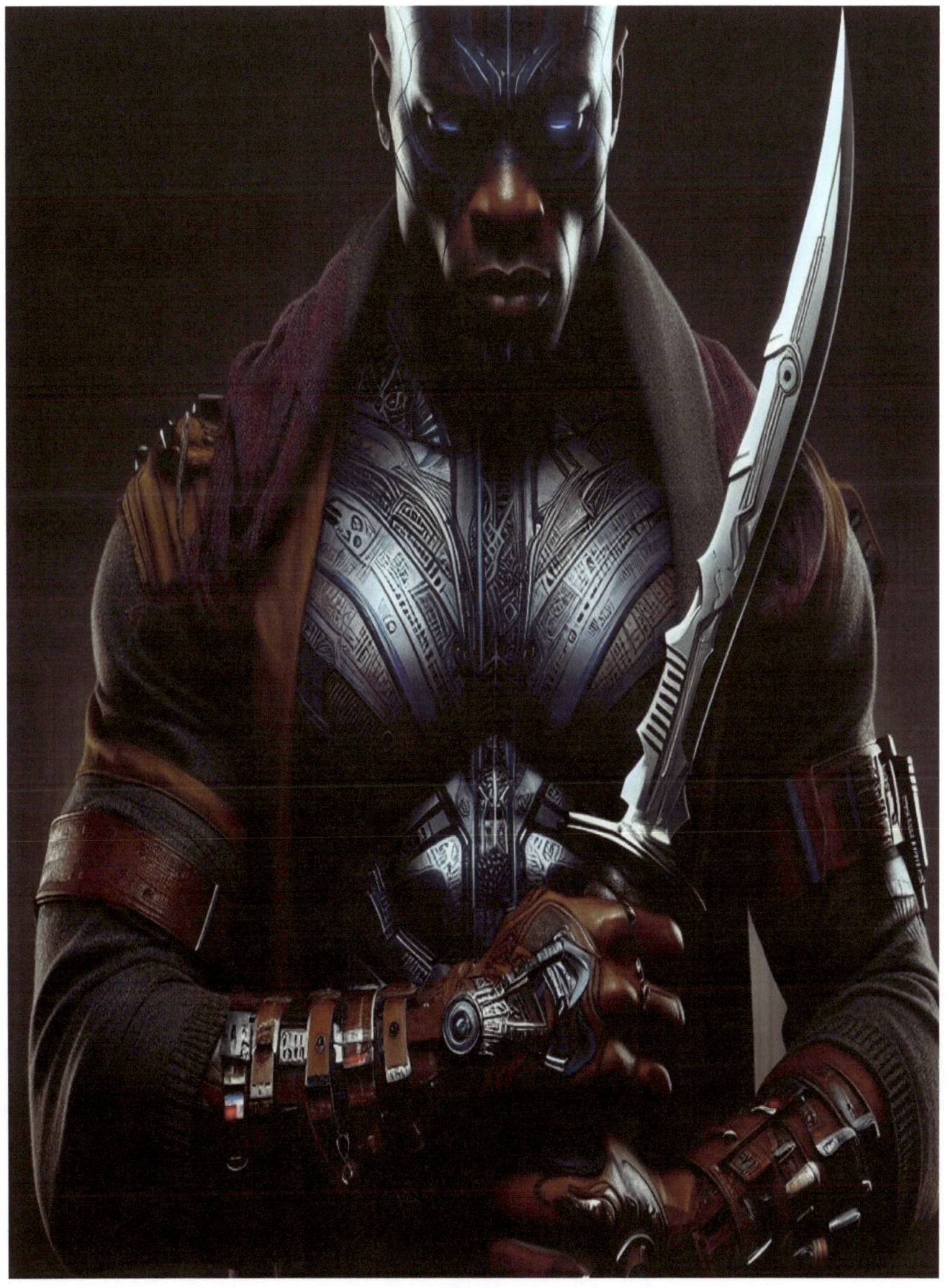

Ogun, while some contribute Ogun's quality to weapons of war his contributions to technology are just as valuable if not more. Ogun's Offerings are catfish, alligator pepper, kola nuts, palm wine and red palm oil, small rats, roosters, salt, snails, tortoise, water, fruit and yams.

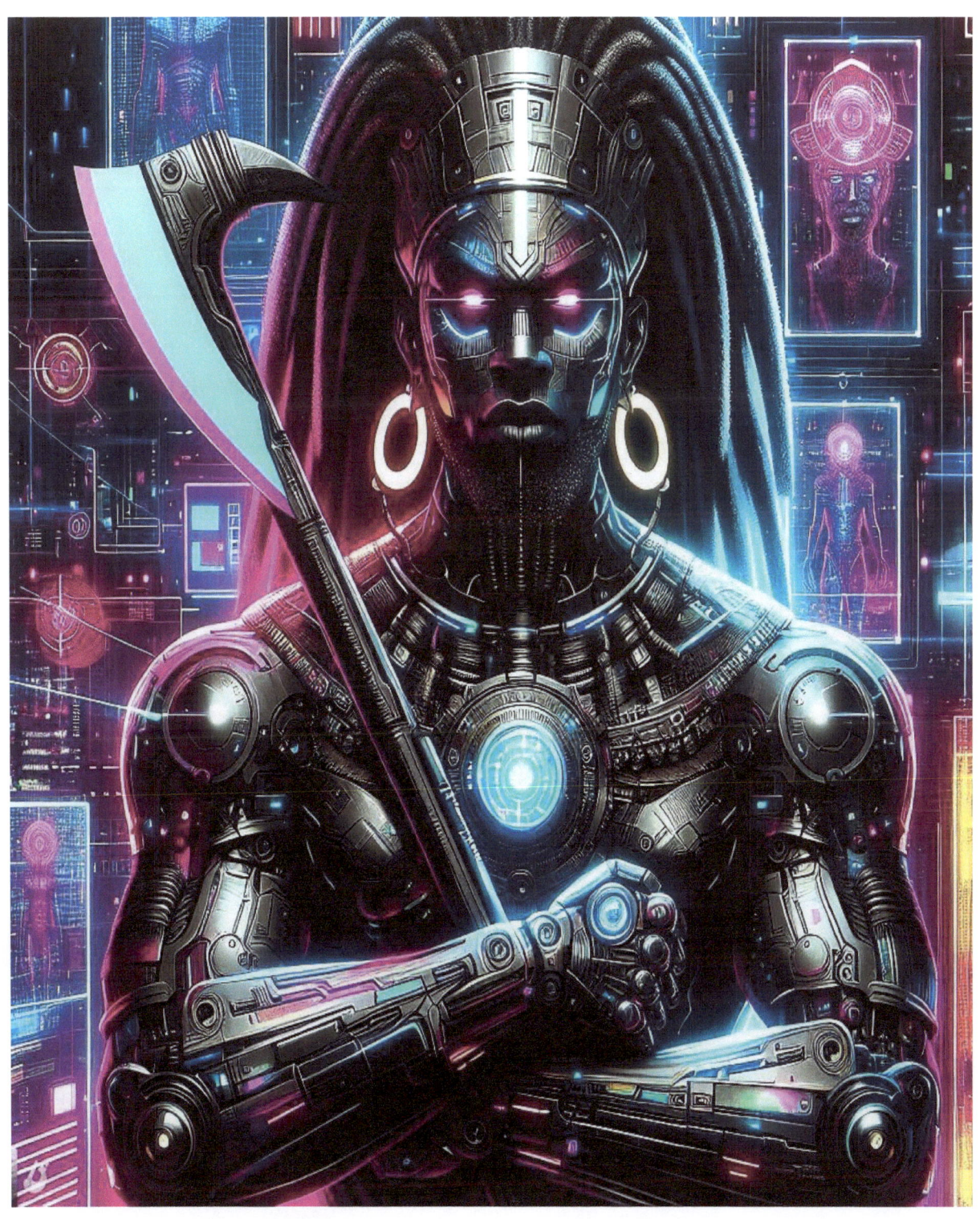

Sage is an antibacterial herb used for culinary, medicinal, and ritual purposes.

While walking through your home repeat these words:

With the cleansing power of this sage, I release all negative energy from this space. May it be filled with light, love, and positive vibrations. As I walk through this sacred smoke, may my body, mind, and spirit be cleansed and renewed.

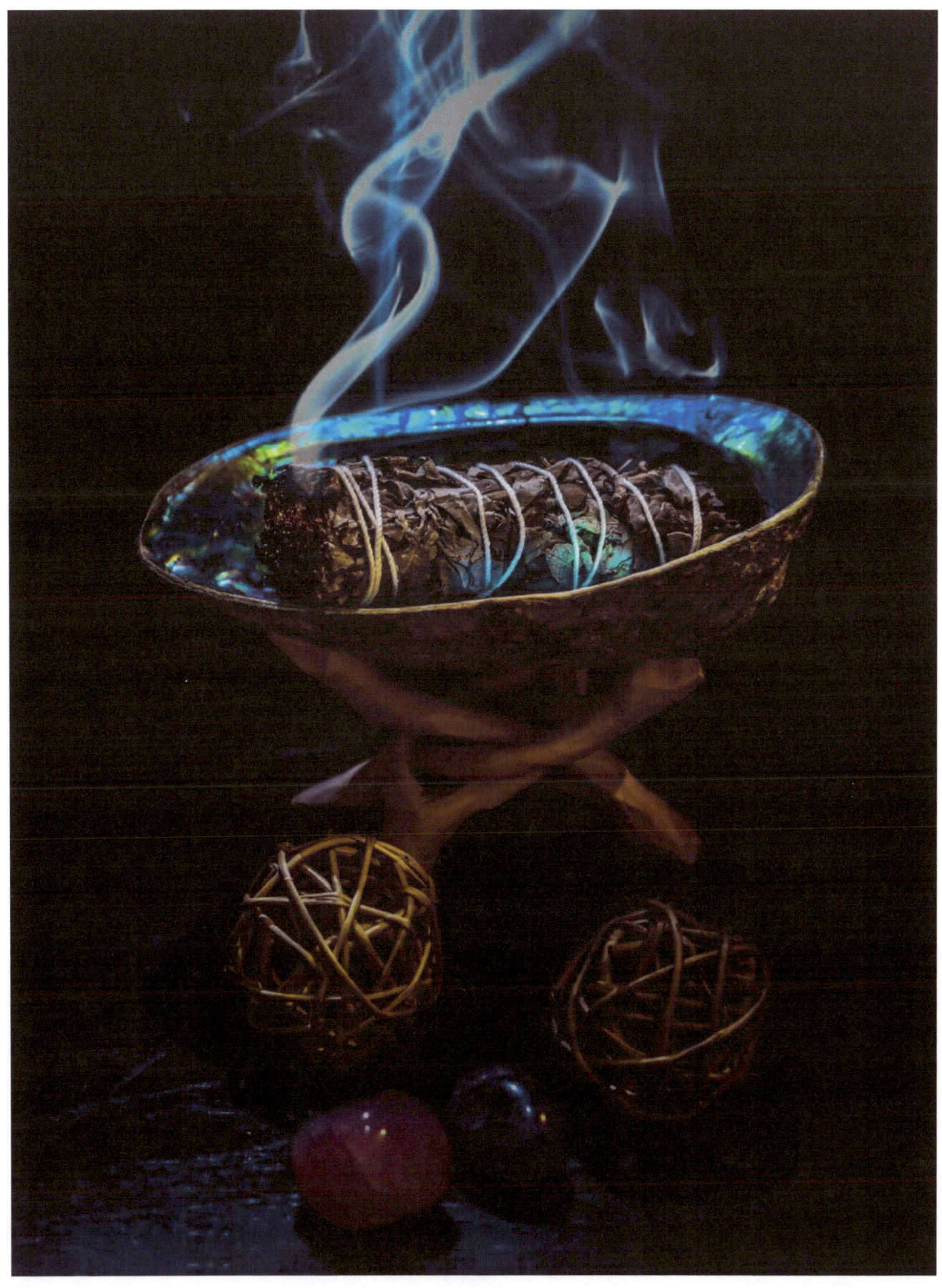

Orishas of the Brown Tree: Past and Future

This coloring book is a Brown Tree Art House Production collaborated between the owners Randale Love and Fonda Rogers. To see more of our artwork look us up on Facebook under Brown Tree Art House or Instagram under Browntree_arthouse. I hope you enjoy your spiritual journey!

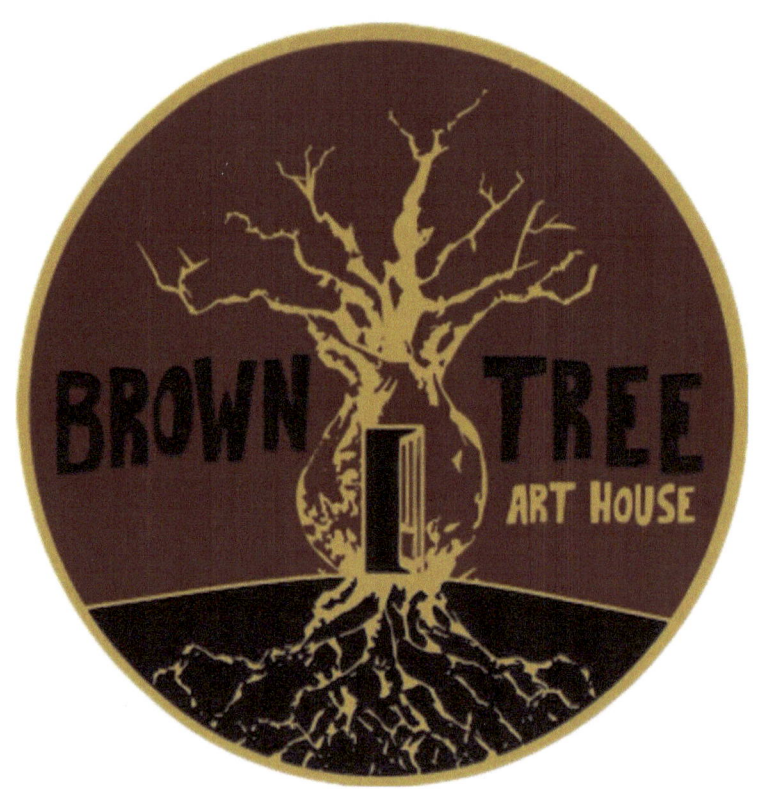